99 THOUGHTS ON LEADING VOLUNTEERS

BY KENT JULIAN

DISCOVER, EQUIP, AND EMPOWER
LEADERS FOR RELATIONAL YOUTH MINISTRY

99 Thoughts on Leading Volunteers
Discover, Equip, and Empower Leaders for Relational Youth Ministry

© 2012 Kent Julian

group.com
simplyyouthministry.com

Credits
Author: Kent Julian
Executive Developer: Nadim Najm
Chief Creative Officer: Joani Schultz
Editor: Rob Cunningham
Art Director: Veronica Preston
Cover Illustration: Amy Hood—Hoodzpah Art & Graphics (wegothoodzpah.com)

Scripture quotations marked NIV are taken from THE HOLY BIBLE, NEW INTERNATIONAL VERSION®, NIV® Copyright © 1973, 1978, 1984, 2011 by Biblica, Inc.™ Used by permission. All rights reserved worldwide.

ISBN 978-0-7644-8284-7

10 9 8 7 6 5 4 3 2 1   20 19 18 17 16 15 14 13 12

Printed in the United States of America.

DEDICATION

This book is dedicated to the incredible volunteers who I was privileged to serve alongside at Christ Community Church in Omaha, Nebraska. You were an amazing team of people, and through you, God did some amazing things!

ACKNOWLEDGMENTS

Thank you to Group and Simply Youth Ministry for the opportunity to write this book. To me, there is nothing greater in youth ministry than equipping and releasing volunteers to impact the lives of teenagers. As Jesus demonstrated in his earthly ministry, equipping and releasing others for ministry is key to multiplying a movement.

Thank you to Rick Lawrence, Andy Brazelton, and Kami Gilmour for your leadership at Group and Simply Youth Ministry. I have great respect for each of you.

Thank you to Dan Glaze. As a volunteer youth worker, you made a huge difference in my life. But not only that, you also served as the model of what a volunteer youth leader should look like in both who you were and what you did.

Thank you to the love of my life, Kathy, and my three amazing kids, Chris, McKenzie, and Kelsey. I love doing life with the four of you!

Kent Julian

TABLE OF CONTENTS

INTRODUCTION

One Overarching Thought...

I've been privileged to experience youth ministry from many different vantage points. I started out as an intern for three summers during college. Once I graduated, I served as a youth pastor in a small-church setting for about five years, after which I served in megachurch settings for almost 10 years before becoming the national youth director of 2,000 affiliated churches across the United States for another seven years. Several years ago I started my own business (liveitforward.com), and with this change came the opportunity to get back to my roots and serve as a volunteer youth leader in my church. Additionally, I have also stayed involved with young people in my community by coaching a 170-member swim team for three months during the summer. I'm with these swimmers Monday through Friday—and, believe it or not, swim team is a more volunteer-intensive endeavor than youth ministry (albeit on a very different level).

Why share these details with you? Simple. I've had the privilege to look at youth ministry from many different angles, and whether my role has been that of an intern, youth pastor, national leader and adviser, swim coach, or volunteer, it's become clear to me that most successes in youth ministry come about because of quality volunteers—and most shortcomings occur because something is lacking with regards to volunteers. As John Maxwell frequently says, "Everything rises and falls with leadership."

Going a bit further, I believe leadership in youth ministry is a bit more nuanced than "everything rises and fall with leadership." In youth ministry, everything rises and falls based on volunteer leadership. More specifically, everything rises and falls based on how well volunteers are recruited, equipped, and released to do the work of the ministry.

To make my point, let me get gut-level honest with you. I know I wasn't the greatest youth pastor on the face of the planet—not even close! I always felt awkward when situations called for me to be "pastoral." What's more, I wasn't the greatest Bible teacher in the world. I didn't have graphic-design skills. I'm not a technological genius. I can't even play guitar! However, looking back, I did one thing right during my years as a youth ministry professional, and that one thing gained me front-row access to seeing God work beyond what I could ever imagine. I was pretty good at cultivating an environment within our ministry that was conducive to discovering, equipping, and empowering adult volunteers for effective youth ministry. This, more than anything else, was the key to the vast majority of success I have witnessed and continue to witness in youth ministry.

What follows are 99 ideas on how to effectively recruit, equip, and release volunteers for youth ministry. By no means is this a comprehensive look at leading volunteers, but I do believe you'll find it a solid read that is well worth your time. If you'd like an opportunity to take a more comprehensive look at what it takes to cultivate an environment within youth ministry that is conducive to discovering, equipping, and empowering adult volunteers for effective youth ministry, why not join me at the next Simply Youth Ministry Conference? I'm usually hosting a couple of "Leading Volunteers" tracks. What's more, there is no better way to be refreshed and renewed for ministry than by attending a Simply Youth Ministry Conference. In a word, it's amazing!

RECRUITING

DISCOVERING AND INVITING VOLUNTEERS TO SERVE IN YOUTH MINISTRY

4 LEADERSHIP THOUGHTS ON THE GREAT COMMISSION

We are called to a gigantic, massive mission, yet it isn't accomplished through gigantic, massive programming. In Jesus' last statement to his disciples—his Great Commission, his graduation speech—he said: *"All authority in heaven and on earth has been given to me. Therefore go and make disciples of all nations, baptizing them in the name of the Father and of the Son and of the Holy Spirit, and teaching them to obey everything I have commanded you. And surely I am with you always, to the very end of the age"* (Matthew 28:18-20 NIV).

01 DISCIPLES AREN'T MADE IN CLASSROOMS

There are a lot of action words in Jesus' commission—go, make disciples, baptize, teach to obey. Yet with all these action words, there is only one phrase that is in the imperative tense, which means there is only one command: "make disciples." All the other words share insights into how to make disciples—make disciples while going about living your life, identify disciples through baptism, and teach disciples to obey all Christ has commanded his followers to be and do. But again, the only command is to "make disciples."

What's a disciple? The biblical meaning is a "learning-follower." This phrase doesn't imply a "pack-50-people-into-a-classroom-to-hear-instructions-on-how-to-live-life-and-then-hope-they-apply-the-lesson" approach. It implies a "learner-who-follows-a-teacher-and-mentor-around-to-learn-from-that-leader" approach. It's time-intensive. It's personal. It is as much mentorship as it is instructional, and it's not something that one leader can do simultaneously with a lot of followers. (Think about it: Jesus is God, and he only took on 12 guys!)

The idea from the start, then, is if you truly want to make disciples of Jesus, you're going to need to focus on cultivating "following" environments instead of just classroom environments.

02 JESUS MODELED DISCIPLE MAKING

By the way, Jesus modeled disciple making. Sure, he did "classroom" stuff. He taught in the temple. There was that Sermon on the Mount gathering. Oh, and he also threw his version of a pizza party with thousands of people. But study the Gospels and you'll see that the majority of his time was spent with the few—the 12, the 70, the 120. In fact, read a harmony of the Gospels (which combines all four Gospels and puts events in chronological order) and you'll discover that the longer Jesus' ministry lasted, the more he ministered in disciple-making environments. It's as if larger gatherings gave people a glimpse of his movement, but he strategically spent the majority of his time in smaller, disciple-making environments where those who were curious and even attracted to his movement could grow as "learning-followers."

0 3 THE APOSTLES FOLLOWED JESUS' LEAD

Jump to the book of Acts and you'll see that the apostles took the "make disciples" commandment of Jesus seriously. Like Jesus, they also led some large-group gatherings, but the vast majority of their focus was on cultivating disciple-making environments. House churches were the primary means of helping learning-followers grow, and let's not fool ourselves into thinking that a 20-minute small group discussion is in the same vein as the house churches in the New Testament. These gatherings allowed Christ-followers to eat together and develop deep relational connections that fostered mentoring and instruction.

(NOTE: We'll talk about how to create similar environments in youth ministry in the Releasing section of this book.)

04 GO AHEAD, STEAL JESUS' IDEA - IT'S NOT PLAGIARISM

So often we read the Gospels and the book of Acts for the message of Christ and altogether miss the methods Jesus and his disciples used to launch Christ's movement. Remember, these five books are historical books, which means they don't teach doctrine as much as they tell a story (besides, Paul was Mr. Doctrine). Therefore, to be good students of historical books, we need to study more than what was said—we need to study what was done. In fact, think of it this way: Doesn't it make sense that if the God of the universe was going to visit earth and spend three and a half years establishing a new movement, then the methods he used to establish that movement and not just the words he said would be worth our study? I think so!

All that to say, the first step to recruiting, equipping, and releasing volunteers in youth ministry is to become students of disciple making ourselves. I strongly encourage you to read a harmony of the Gospel with an eye toward the methods Jesus and his apostles used to launch and grow Christ's movement. Additionally, one of the best books on disciple making that I've ever read is an oldie, but a goodie: *With Christ in the School of Disciple Making* by Carl Wilson. It's a heady read, but a good read.

❸ BIG-PICTURE IDEAS ABOUT RECRUITING VOLUNTEERS

0️⃣5️⃣ DON'T DO IT!

I don't like recruiting volunteers. In fact, I HATE it!

Hate is a strong word, and that's why I'm intentionally using it here. I hate begging and arm-twisting. I hate negotiating terms of agreement. I hate trying to convince someone that youth ministry is a worthy calling.

So I simply don't do it. That's right, I don't recruit. Tried it once and will never do it again.

While I use the word *recruiting* in the heading to this section, I do so only because it's a word that everyone in youth ministry understands. But please hear me load and clear: I don't recruit volunteers and neither should you—at least not in the way most youth leaders would define recruiting. Therefore, from here on out, when I use the word *recruit* in a positive sense, please know that I'm using it very differently than how most youth leaders use it. In fact, the following two ideas will give you a clearer picture of what I mean when I use the term *recruit*.

06   PEOPLE HATE TO BE SOLD

Because I'm a business owner, 80 percent of my job is marketing my company's services and products. If I don't market, my family doesn't eat. It's that simple.

There are a lot of different methods I could use to market my company, some of which I hate as much as I hate recruiting volunteers. I have come to discover that the marketing methods I hate the most have a common denominator with many of the typical approaches used by youth pastors to recruit volunteers: *push selling*. Push selling involves "pushing" people into buying something they really don't want to buy. Think of it as interrupting a person at dinner and jamming a huge billboard-size sign in his face that reads "BUY NOW" even though that person couldn't care less about what you are selling. That's push selling, and it doesn't work particularly well, especially in the long run, because it creates dissatisfied buyers, yields multiple refund requests, and ruins a company's reputation.

When it comes to looking for volunteers, a good rule of thumb is this: If an approach feels like push selling, push as far away from that approach as possible.

07 PEOPLE LOVE TO BUY

With that said, you still have to "market" to volunteers. If you don't, you can't feed the youth ministry family God has called you to lead. So here's another big-picture rule of thumb to keep in mind when inviting volunteers to serve in youth ministry:

People love to buy IF they see their purchase as a positive investment.

For instance, I love to buy Mac® products. Why? Because they enhance the effectiveness and efficiency of both my life and work. I also love buying good running shoes. Why? Because they allow me to participate in one of my favorite activities: running.

The process of discovering and inviting people to buy into something that they view as a positive investment is called *pull selling*, and pull selling requires the highest form of marketing. The focus of this marketing is to authentically serve prospects by providing them with information about a service or product that you believe will truly add value to their lives, and then when they fully understand the information, provide them with the opportunity to buy into the service or product. No manipulation. No over-the-top pressure. No heavy-handed tactics. It's all about authentically serving others in a way that you believe will add value to their lives.

If they don't feel pulled to your offer, then no sale is pushed.

I don't know about you, but pull selling sounds a lot like a big-picture concept to embrace when recruiting volunteers.

DO'S AND DON'TS FOR RECRUITING VOLUNTEERS

Now that we've spelled out some big-picture concepts about recruiting volunteers, let's flesh them out into specific do's and don'ts.

08 DON'T MAKE CHURCH-WIDE ANNOUNCEMENTS

The absolutely worst approach to recruiting volunteers is to make church-wide announcements either from the platform or in the bulletin. If I was a betting man, I would bet a million bucks that the one person in your congregation who is least qualified to work with teenagers will volunteer.

09 DO WINE AND DINE

Have you ever been recruited for a high-end job? It's a 180-degree different experience from applying for a job. When you apply for a job, you're likely competing against dozens of applicants and your job is to convince the employer to hire you. On the other hand, if a company recruits you, the tables are turned and it's their job to convince you to take the position. In this scenario, you don't wine and dine the employer—the employer wines and dines you!

When I find quality people that I believe would be good volunteers in youth ministry, it's my job to wine and dine them. But my approach is part wine and dine, part courting. Let me explain.

First, I usually invite the person out for a cup of coffee just to let him know what I see in him. The conversation involves me explaining the specific character traits and skills I see that I believe would be a good fit for youth ministry. This is not an "ask," which is a major mistake many youth pastors make. Telling someone they'd be good in youth ministry and immediately following those words with a sign-on-the-dotted-line "ask" is similar to a marriage proposal on a first date. Most potential volunteers will be surprised that you think they are qualified to work with teenagers; therefore, the best approach is to have an initial conversation and just let your words sink in. Remember, we want to pull, not push; this means we need to proceed one step at a time.

The next step is to take this person out for a meal to answer his questions, as well as to give details of what being a volunteer involves. This is usually when you want to make the "ask."

I call this approach wining and dining for several reasons. First, you are pursuing people. Second, it works best if these meetings are done over coffee or a meal instead of in an office or the church hallway. A meal lets a person know that you value him and that the discussion is important. Third, while this approach takes time and costs a bit of your budget, the end results are worth the investment. I don't have any hard stats, but I know my ROI—my return on investment—of people who said yes to volunteering went way up once I started using this pull selling approach over my former push selling strategy.

10 DON'T WINE AND DINE THE OPPOSITE SEX ALONE

I never allow myself to be alone with the opposite sex. My thinking here isn't just to protect me from temptation or the appearance of evil; it's primarily to honor my wife and let her know I deeply value our relationship.

11 DO WINE AND DINE THE OPPOSITE SEX WITH OTHERS

Even though I don't allow myself to be alone with members of the opposite sex, I still want the way I recruit to demonstrate that I value them. Therefore, when recruiting women to serve as volunteers, I usually recruit several at one time and take someone along with me. Or even better, if there is a key female leader I believe will represent the youth ministry well, I involve her in the recruiting process.

12 DON'T FOCUS ON TALENT OVER CHARACTER

"Man, I really need a worship leader, and Chris can flat out play the guitar!" I put Chris on the worship team, and soon he had taken on a strong leadership role with that team. There was only one problem—I later discovered Chris was sleeping with his girlfriend. In leadership, the best talent can never cover up or hide major character flaws.

13 DO EMPHASIZE CHARACTER OVER TALENT

After my experience with Chris and several other volunteers, I started using this four-quadrant chart to help me make decisions regarding recruiting volunteers. I never recruit potential volunteers if I believe they fall on the left side of the chart, but I always recruit people on the right side. The reason? Most talents and skills can be taught and developed, but a person's attitude and character can only be shaped from within. If a person does not have the right attitude and character to begin with, I don't trust that person to invest in the lives of the teenagers.

NEVER RECRUIT	ALWAYS RECRUIT
Limited Talent and Skills Poor Character and Attitude	Limited Talent and Skills Great Character and Attitude
Great Talent and Skills Poor Character and Attitude	Great Talent and Skills Great Character and Attitude

14 DON'T LIMIT RECRUITING VOLUNTEERS TO ONCE A YEAR

"Wow, you sure would be a great youth ministry volunteer, but it's February and we only take on new volunteers in August." Sorry, wrong answer!

15 DO HAVE SEASONS WHEN RECRUITING VOLUNTEERS IS A PRIORITY

While I'll invite people to be volunteers at any time during the year, recruiting is my No. 1 priority during the summer. In fact, in larger church settings, from May to August, recruiting new volunteers usually took 50 percent of my time. That might sound like a huge time commitment, but this approach is why our ministry was able to keep approximately a one-volunteer-to-four-student ratio even when our ministry grew to 500-600 students.

16 DON'T RECRUIT VOLUNTEERS ON YOUR OWN

Your No. 1 resource for names of potential volunteers is your current volunteer staff because they know what is required for volunteering. Therefore, it's wise to tap into this resource.

Here's how I did it. At the end of every school year, I had my volunteer team complete an evaluation. The first two questions on that evaluation were the most important questions:

- Do you plan to volunteer again next year?

- Who do you know that you think would be a great volunteer? (I asked for three or four names from each volunteer, but the more the merrier.)

When I made contact with the names I received from my team of volunteers, I explained that "so-and-so is currently a volunteer and said that she thinks you'd be a good volunteer, too."

17 DO MOST OF THE RECRUITING YOURSELF

I've seen volunteer job descriptions that include this line: "We expect you to recruit at least one other volunteer this year." In my opinion, this is a mistake. Most volunteers are not good recruiters. What's more, most don't want to bother with it. That's why I ask them for names, and then I do the recruiting myself or with a select team of others who enjoy recruiting and are actually gifted at it.

18 DON'T OVERDO THE JOB DESCRIPTION

I'll explain volunteer job descriptions in Section Two, but for now let me share two quick thoughts about volunteer job descriptions (in other words, ministry descriptions). First, you need them! How can a prospective volunteer make an informed decision about serving if she doesn't know what is expected of her? Second, don't overdo it. Most volunteers can serve three to seven hours a week, yet many volunteer job descriptions, if followed, would require 10 to 12 hours a week. This is one of those times to keep it as simple and straightforward as possible.

19 DO CLEARLY COMMUNICATE WHAT IS EXPECTED

While you don't want to overdo it on a volunteer job description, you also don't want to drop the ball on clearly communicating what is expected. I have found that the best volunteer job descriptions focus on three or four primary responsibilities (again, more on this in Section Two). This allows for focused training and clear accountability.

20 DON'T REQUIRE A LIFETIME COMMITMENT

Volunteers are like contract employees. What I mean is they need a definite starting date and a definite ending date. The reason is two-fold:

- Clear starting and ending dates help with recruiting. People are more likely to sign on the dotted line if they know their commitment isn't forever.

- A clear ending date allows both parties to re-evaluate how well the current agreement is working. If everything is going well, then committing to another season of ministry can occur. If there are issues on either end, those things can be worked through and the appropriate decision can be made.

21 DO REQUIRE A YEARLONG COMMITMENT

While requiring a lifetime commitment is too much, you don't want too short of a commitment either. The reason is because investing in the lives of teenagers and shepherding them is more like a marathon than a sprint, so a minimum of a school year should be required. The goal, of course, is that volunteers will recommit at the end of each school year, but if that doesn't work out, then at least the volunteer will be moving out during the time when other transitions are taking place.

22 DON'T REQUIRE WEEK-IN AND WEEK-OUT SERVICE

Sharp volunteers usually have a lot on their plate. Jobs. Kids. Other ministry commitments. Personal development experiences. There are a few "Super Volunteers" who can be at every activity and don't understand why five more weekly events aren't planned, but if we work most volunteers week-in and week-out without a break, we won't keep them around very long.

23 DO SCHEDULE BREAKS INTO YOUR MINISTRY CALENDAR

I have found that volunteers tend to recommit to service year-in and year-out if I schedule breaks into the annual youth ministry calendar. I have also found that they tend to serve with more enthusiasm and passion when I schedule breaks throughout the year. Think about it— even if you love your job, you need time off. Weekends and vacations actually allow you to get re-energized and dive back into work with more effectiveness.

In the same way, I think "weekends" and "vacation" when putting together my annual youth ministry calendar. For me, "weekends" revolve around series. For instance, let's say your small group program occurs on Sunday evenings. If that's the case, a good way to schedule in "weekend" breaks is to plan three- to five-week series, and when each series is over, take the following Sunday night off.

When it comes to "vacation" breaks, I have found a short vacation and a long vacation during the ministry year are most helpful. During the Christmas season, I shut down programming for three or four weeks. There is so much going on church-wide during that season anyway that it just seems like a natural time for a break. Additionally, I give my volunteer team the entire summer off, and this break is the one that really causes my volunteers to recommit year after year. By the end of a long ministry year, they are tired, and a three-month break is exactly what they need!

I know these suggestions go against conventional wisdom, and honestly, I hear many youth leaders gasp when I share these thoughts at live events. Let me share the conventional wisdom I've heard, along with what I have discovered to be reality.

Conventional Wisdom: If you don't meet every week, students will eventually stop coming.

Reality: If you take breaks after each series, attendance increases. There are a multitude of reasons why this is true, including the fact that volunteers serve with more energy and passion when they get an occasional break, which means they connect better with students. Additionally, even students enjoy breaks and seem to come back with more energy for the next series.

Conventional Wisdom: You need MORE volunteers during the summer, not fewer.

Reality. If you are focused and intentional, you can run summer programming with just a handful of volunteers. Here's how we've done it:

- First, we always cut back to one weekly, big-group program that doesn't revolve around small groups. This allows us to run a regular gathering with just a handful of volunteers.

- Second, we do several "hangout" gatherings. These are easy-to-plan activities, and volunteers can show up if they'd like to simply connect with teenagers.

- Finally, instead of trying to cram in as many events as possible during the summer, we have just one major event (usually some sort of major mission or ministry trip). Our goal is to make this a topnotch experience, so we build weeks of training around the trip, and this training ends up taking up most of the summer. We also recruit a team of adult volunteers just for this trip, and because it's so focused, it's not difficult to find quality people to serve. What all this means is that the students who take part in this opportunity end up with a very unique experience that is as deep and intentional, if not more so, than the small group ministry they experience during the school year.

24 ANY AGE CAN SERVE

Most youth leaders, whether intentionally or unintentionally, limit their team to an age bracket of 20 years—10 years below their age to 10 years above their age. If you fall for this trap, you'll miss out on some amazing volunteers.

25 HIGH SCHOOL STUDENTS

I believe high school students, especially seniors, can serve as volunteers in middle school ministry. Obviously, I do not want to take these teenagers away from the high school group, so I only allow them to serve during times when the high school group is not meeting. Additionally, I usually have them serve alongside adults, especially if they are helping to lead a small group.

The biggest potential roadblock to effective ministry for people in this season of life: immaturity.

26 YOUNG ADULT VOLUNTEERS

Younger volunteers such as college students, young adults, and young married couples have a lot to offer your volunteer team. They often have more time to serve. They usually understand youth culture a bit better because they are not too far removed from it. They can also serve as "big brother" and "big sister" role models.

The biggest potential roadblock to effective ministry for people in this season of life: trying to be a teenager's buddy.

27 PARENT VOLUNTEERS

Volunteers who happen to be parents also have a lot to offer. While they usually don't have as much time as younger volunteers and won't understand youth culture as well, they tend to be more mature and have greater life experience. They can do a great job serving as wise mentors and even can be positive parent figures for teenagers, which is so needed today.

The biggest potential roadblock to effective ministry for people in this season of life: being overbearing and being too much of a "parent."

28 SENIOR VOLUNTEERS

Volunteers who are empty nesters or retired are the most untapped resource in our churches. Like younger volunteers, they often have more time to serve than parents do.

And while they are usually light years removed from youth culture, most have incredible life experiences that they could share with teenagers.

The biggest potential roadblock to effective ministry for people in this season of life: the belief that teenagers don't want them to be part of their lives.

CREATIVE PLACES TO FIND VOLUNTEERS

As already stated, the best resource for recruiting new volunteers is your current team of volunteers. However, if you need to find additional volunteers or if you are starting from scratch and don't have any volunteers, here are a few creative ideas that have worked well for me.

29 IF YOU ARE STARTING FROM SCRATCH

If you are starting from scratch, remember: Do NOT just make a church-wide announcement that you need volunteers. Instead, take time to get to know people in your church and pursue those who fit the type of volunteer you need. If you strategically start out slow with programming and don't overcrowd your calendar, you'll likely find several great prospects within the four walls of your church upon whom to build the foundation of your volunteer team.

30 TAP INTO LOCAL COLLEGES

I've found local colleges to be a great place to find additional volunteers. At the beginning of the school year, both Christian and secular colleges usually do some sort of "ministry" or "service" fair in which outside organizations can represent themselves to college students. For me, becoming an official organization with the college allowed our ministry to set up booths during the fair days, and working those booths proved highly fruitful for recruiting volunteers.

31 TAP INTO YOUTH MINISTRY MAJORS

If you do have a Christian college nearby, network with the head of the youth ministry department. This one connection could lead to volunteers, interns, and who knows what else!

32 PARTNER WITH LOCAL PARACHURCH ORGANIZATIONS

When I was in a smaller church, our ministry grew so fast that we could not fully staff ourselves with people from within the walls of our church. So we partnered with a local parachurch organization—I provided leadership for their program, and our ministry picked up a few additional volunteers for our programming as well. Of course, I had to clear this with my church board, but after all the details were worked out, this approach helped our group continue to grow and allowed us to continue to stay true to our one-volunteer-for-every-four-teenagers goal.

REHEARSING

TRAINING & EQUIPPING VOLUNTEERS TO SERVE IN YOUTH MINISTRY

7 REASONS TO TRAIN VOLUNTEERS

OK, let's start with the basics. Have you ever thought about why you train and equip volunteers in the first place? Surprisingly, when I ask this question at youth ministry training conferences, a blank stare usually emerges across the faces of attendees. At first the stare is an "are you kidding me" glare; but it often evolves into a "you know, I'm not too sure" gaze.

As leaders, if we're fuzzy about why we train and equip volunteers, our volunteers will be in the dark as to why we do it or, even worse, what we're trying to accomplish. So here are seven reasons that will shine a bright light on why equipping volunteers is a must.

33 CONNECTING WITH THE BIG PICTURE

There is no better way to communicate the big picture of youth ministry (purpose, core values, programs) than face-to-face time with your entire volunteer team. Youth ministry handbooks are great, PowerPoint® presentations are great—but nothing beats communicating vision better than gathering everyone together for eyeball-to-eyeball conversations.

❸❹ LANGUAGE LESSONS

Regular training allows a volunteer team to develop a common vocabulary and define important terms. Speaking the same language helps team members combat the problem of talking past one another.

❸❺ COMMUNICATION

Communication with volunteers—no, overcommunication—is essential to success in youth ministry. Newsletters, weekly announcements, text messages—all are great; but again, nothing beats face-to-face communication. Why? Because face-to-face time

creates opportunities for feedback, and it
shapes ideas and strategy.

36 SKILL DEVELOPMENT

Most volunteers need "how-to" help with
things like developing relationships with
teenagers, leading small groups, counseling
students, spiritually challenging teenagers,
and more. Significant parts of training should
be dedicated to just that—training!

37 REHEARSING

I titled this section "Rehearsing" because
the vast majority of volunteer training is
knowledge-based rather than experientially
based. Yet the one thing that volunteers need
most is the opportunity to practice what they
are taught. This can be done through activities
such as role-playing, but even better, it can be
done through hands-on equipping strategies

as well (see the Hands-On Equipping Grid piece that immediately follows this list).

38 ACCOUNTABILITY

Training meetings provide an excellent opportunity for ministry team members to hold themselves accountable to the vision of the ministry, as well as to one another.

39 FRIENDSHIPS

One of the best things about being involved in youth ministry is the development of life-long friendships. Training meetings, especially when hosted in a relaxed environment, cultivate the opportunity for friendship roots to grow deep.

HANDS-ON EQUIPPING GRID

Classroom training is good, but in-the-trenches equipping is significantly better. Classroom training is theory, but in-the-trenches equipping is theory fleshed out in reality. Classroom training is knowledge-based, but in-the-trenches equipping incorporates knowledge with experience. Both classroom training and in-the-trenches equipping are needed, but a heavier emphasis should be given to in-the-trenches equipping. However, the reality is that most, if not all, volunteer training falls into the classroom training variety.

The best way to flip the switch and put more emphasis on in-the-trenches equipping is to create a "Hands-On Equipping Grid" for training new volunteers. Here's a simple example of what we did with our middle school small group leaders to create a Hands-On Equipping Grid:

40 YOU WATCH ME

At the start of a new ministry season (usually in August), we paired new small group leaders with veteran small group leaders during our kick-off volunteer training gatherings. This provided new leaders with a go-to person for all questions and concerns. This ended up being the key in helping new leaders adjust to our ministry without feeling overwhelmed or thrown to the wolves. It also allowed veteran leaders to grow in their own leadership and ownership of the ministry.

Additionally, once we kicked off our small groups, new leaders and their groups met together with the veteran leader's group for the first series or two. During the first couple of sessions of the first series, the new small group leader would simply watch the veteran leader lead the group. Afterward, they discussed what was done and why, and the veteran leader would answer any questions the new leader had.

41 WE DO IT TOGETHER

Once the new small group leader felt ready,
she would lead half of the small group session
herself. Again, after each session, the two
leaders discussed the ins and outs of what
happened during small group. The veteran
leader encouraged the new leader with things
that worked well and made suggestions for
things that could be improved.

42 I WATCH YOU

Near the end of the first small group series
or at the beginning of the second, the new
leader would plan and lead the entire small
group meeting herself while the veteran leader
observed. The new leader did this at least a
couple of times, and each time the veteran
leader would meet afterward with her to
encourage her and review the evening.

43 YOU DO IT YOURSELF

By the end of the first or second small group series, the new leader felt fully equipped. The hands-on experience gained during the first series or two gave her the confidence and skills needed to lead a small group on her own. What's more, she also had an established relationship with a veteran leader in case she had a question or needed help during her first year as a volunteer.

44 YOU TRAIN SOMEONE ELSE

The No. 1 benefit of this Hands-On Equipping Grid is that it equips new leaders right from the start through in-the-trenches experiences. Instead of trying to navigate leadership with head knowledge alone, new leaders gained both head knowledge and practical skills in a very short amount of time.

But another valuable benefit is the leadership multiplication that occurs because of this approach. Every year, we had more leaders of leaders—more volunteers who were equipped to train new leaders. What's more, these leaders naturally felt more ownership in our ministry.

THE PARETO PRINCIPLE AND SHEPHERDING MINISTRY

You have probably heard that 20 percent of church attendees do 80 percent of the work or that 20 percent of church attendees give 80 percent of the money, but did you know these figures are based on an actual principle? The Pareto Principle (also known as the 80/20 rule) states that 20 percent of our efforts and/or 20 percent of people produce 80 percent of the results in practically every arena of life. Think about it—we know this is true in church, but did you realize that approximately 20 percent of people pay 80 percent of taxes? It turns out that 20 percent of a company's sales team makes 80 percent of the sales. Even more, 20 percent of a company's products and services bring in 80 percent of its revenue. If you need more convincing, go look in your closet—I guarantee that you wear 20 percent of your clothes 80 percent of the time!

Have you ever thought about using the Pareto Principle to your advantage with volunteers?

45 WHAT 20 PERCENT OF MINISTRY EFFORTS LEADS TO 80 PERCENT OF LIFE-CHANGE?

Clearly relational ministry is the 20 percent of ministry efforts that leads to 80 percent of life-change in the lives of teenagers. So doesn't it make sense that we should be extremely intentional about getting our volunteers involved in relational ministry? I think so! In fact, I've been so intentional about it, I've come up with a term for it: shepherding ministry. I want each volunteer to intentionally be shepherding four to five teenagers.

46 THE MOST IMPORTANT PARETO PRINCIPLE QUESTION FOR VOLUNTEERS

If intentional shepherding ministry leads to 80 percent of the life-change that happens in students, youth ministry leadership needs to ask itself one very important question:

How can we dedicate enough time and effort to shepherding ministry so that we can multiple the opportunity for life-change?

47 DEDICATE 80 PERCENT OF THE VOLUNTEER TEAM TO SHEPHERDING MINISTRY

One way to dedicate more time and effort to shepherding ministry is to turn the Pareto Principle on its head and give 80 percent of your time and focus to the 20-percent efforts in ministry that lead to 80 percent of life-change in teenagers. You might need to read that again to make sure you catch what I'm saying.

For instance, you could dedicate 80 percent of your volunteer team to shepherding ministry roles like leading small groups. This is the approach we took at one of the larger churches I served. Out of our 120 volunteers, the vast majority of them were exclusively serving as small group leaders. In fact, as you'll see in the volunteer job description piece that follows, if a volunteer had five to seven hours a week to give to youth ministry, all of those hours were given to shepherding the teenagers in their group. We did not expect that person to serve in other areas of ministry or even show up for other programs. Therefore, 80 percent of the time and focus of our volunteer team was given to the 20 percent of our efforts (in other words, small groups) that we believed would lead to 80 percent of the life-change we saw in teenagers.

As a side note, we quickly discovered that we could effectively run all of our programming (such as music, event planning and implementation, up-front teaching) with 20 percent of our volunteer team or less as long as we had parents helping out with food, driving, crowd control, and other similar needs. For us, it was a no-brainer to use "nonvolunteers" for simple tasks that, in the past, took up the time and focus of the majority of our volunteers, in order to free up 80 percent of our volunteers for total focus on shepherding ministry.

4⑧ DEDICATE 80 PERCENT OF VOLUNTEERS' TIME TO SHEPHERDING MINISTRY

The other way to dedicate 80 percent of our efforts to shepherding ministry is to empower volunteers to devote 80 percent of their time and energy to roles like leading small groups. This is the approach we took in the smaller church I served. Because we only had a handful of volunteers, each of us had to be involved in a ministry task according to our giftedness. For instance, I focused on teaching, someone else focused on details and administration, someone else led music—you get the point. One of my major jobs as the leader of this group was to make sure that no volunteers put their ministry task before shepherding ministry, so I was always encouraging and challenging team members to give the vast majority of their time to relational ministry.

VOLUNTEER JOB DESCRIPTIONS

The best way I know to make sure 80 percent of our volunteers' efforts go to shepherding ministry is to create a volunteer job description (ministry description) that clearly communicates this reality. For the sake of simplicity, here is the volunteer job description we created for small group leaders in the larger church context I mentioned above. Remember, their role was shepherding ministry—that's it! Notice the simplicity and clarity of this ministry description.

4⑨ OBJECTIVE STATEMENT

I wanted these volunteers to know they had one objective and one objective only: *to cultivate an environment that is conducive to the spiritual and holistic development of a small group of teenagers within our ministry.*

50 ACCOUNTABILITY

Here are the two big ideas we held these volunteers accountable for doing in the lives of teenagers in order to meet the objective statement:

- Connecting with the teenagers you shepherd in such a way that you earn the right to speak into their lives.

- Speaking God's grace and truth into the lives of the teenagers you shepherd by the way you live, the way you interact with them, and the way you lead your small group.

51 ROLES

Specifically, here are the three roles/priorities we asked these volunteers to pursue in order to connect with the teenagers they shepherded and to speak God's grace and truth into their lives.

Because we knew that most volunteers could give us five to seven hours each week, we even spelled out the amount of time we asked them to dedicate to each role.

- **Prayer** – We asked shepherding volunteers to commit their first 30 minutes of volunteer time each week to specifically pray for each teenager in their small group. The reason? Life-change is a spiritual process! As a side note, in the Releasing section of this book, I share a tool called "Connection Journals" that supercharged this role for volunteers (see Thought 90).

- **Intentional Relationships** – Shepherding volunteers were asked to commit their next 60 to 120 minutes to activities that helped them build relationships with their group members—attending school events, grabbing coffee at Starbucks®, whatever. By the way, there was no way these volunteers could commit an hour or two each week to building relationships with the teenagers in their small group if we expected them to be involved in other programming; they simply didn't have enough time.

- **Communicating God's Grace and Truth** – Finally, shepherding sponsors were asked to commit their last three to five hours preparing for and leading their small group. We actually taught these leaders how to prepare a transformational Bible study in two hours or less, something else I share in the Releasing section of this book (see Thought 93).

CALENDAR-AT-A-GLANCE

Before discussing the importance of different training seasons with volunteers, a few thoughts about a youth ministry calendar should be addressed.

52 NEW YEAR'S DOESN'T START IN JANUARY

New Year's Day might be January 1, but on most youth ministry calendars, New Year's Day needs to be connected with the beginning of school. The launch of school is the best time to launch new ministry initiatives or restart old ones because it's the time of the year when teenagers and families are getting back into the swing of their routines. This means there is more energy and focus for launching new things in the fall than at any other time of the year. Additionally, there is more of a runway to get new programs off the ground because everything is pretty nonstop from the start of school until Christmas. After that, the year gets broken up much more randomly.

53 A YEAR IN ADVANCE

Want a guaranteed way to put major chips in your pocket with volunteers, parents, elders, board members, the senior pastor, and all the other powers-that-be? When August rolls around, have your ministry calendar for the new school year (August through May) mapped out. Not only does this make you look like a true professional who takes the position seriously, but it also helps both volunteers and parents plan and schedule their year accordingly. In fact, I have found that both volunteers and parents are more committed to the youth ministry when they feel like I respect them enough to let them know in advance what's happening.

5 SEASONS OF TRAINING

There are four seasons to the calendar year, but did you know there are five seasons to the volunteer training calendar? This is especially true with volunteers who serve in shepherding roles.

54 COMMUNICATION KICKOFF (AUGUST)

The start of the ministry year is a great time to gather all volunteers together and get everyone on the same page. And by all means, make it a big deal! Get away on a retreat together. Develop a special program. Do whatever you can to start the year off strong and let your volunteers know how important they are to the youth ministry.

In one church where I led, we hosted a half-day gathering for all new volunteers in order to train them in the purpose, values, philosophy, and programs of our ministry.

Then we hosted two nights to kick off training for all volunteers. The first night included a dinner and hilarious programming to introduce our ministry theme for the year (think SNL meets Purpose-Driven Youth Ministry). We also broke into teams so new volunteers could get to know their mentoring volunteers. The second night was more nuts-and-bolts training and planning for launching the ministry.

55 CONNECT (SEPTEMBER-OCTOBER)

Once we launched small groups in September, the first couple of months of volunteer training were dedicated to equipping volunteers in how to relationally connect with teenagers in their group. The "Hands-On Equipping Grid" explained earlier really helped this process (see Thoughts 40-44).

56 CONTENT (NOVEMBER-DECEMBER)

By October, small groups settled into
their rhythm and our volunteer training
focused on equipping leaders to prepare a
transformational small group experience.
Half the training was dedicated to teaching
how-to details; the other half was dedicated
to veteran volunteers and new volunteers
preparing a couple of lessons together so
that new volunteers actually had a chance
to rehearse the process a couple of times
(again, part of the "Hands-On Equipping Grid"
explained in Thoughts 40-44).

57 CHALLENGE (JANUARY-APRIL)

Once January hit, training became really
exciting. Our goal was for every shepherding
volunteer to personally challenge each
teenager in their small group regarding one
spiritual roadblock (something the volunteer
believed was hindering the teenager's

relationship with Christ) and one spiritual opportunity (a positive step the teenager could take that the volunteer believed would help the teenager's relationship with Christ). I'll explain this process more in the Releasing section of the book (see Thoughts 91-92), but notice how the focus of volunteer training moved from a skills/content emphasis to an actual shepherding focus through the school year. What's more, this season of equipping had very few up-front, content-based training elements to it; instead, it was volunteers sitting in teams specifically talking about how to spiritually challenge different teenagers in their groups. This not only helped us zero in on equipping and releasing volunteers to do the type of ministry we said we valued, it also kept training fresh and engaging because it dealt with actual ministry that was taking place.

REHEARSING

58 CELE-BREAK-TION (MAY)

As small groups came to a close, we would throw a Cele-break-tion party for our volunteers. We celebrated what God had done in our ministry that year, we celebrated volunteers' service to the ministry, we made sure they helped us evaluate the ministry, and then we gave them a break from ministry (as stated earlier in Thought 23, most of our volunteers took the summer off).

WHEN LEADING CHANGE, FAST IS SLOW AND SLOW IS FAST

When it comes to making major changes in youth ministry, many youth leaders end up losing volunteers because they believe change must be made at hyper-speed. Wise leaders realize that significant change requires thought, planning, and time to implement correctly. What's more, wise leaders understand two important facts about leading change:

- Change actually happens faster when we are willing to slow down on the front end of change

- Our greatest asset when making a change is the volunteer team

59 THE TIMING OF CHANGE

Want a surefire way to make a lot of people unhappy? Make a major change in the middle of the school year—like January. This is mistake *numero uno* made by most youth pastors, yet they always seem surprised when volunteers and parents get upset. Well, allow me to enlighten you since I'm now both a volunteer and a parent of teenagers.

By the time January rolls around, everything about our family has a well-established rhythm to it. What's more, we have made a lot of other commitments outside of youth ministry that also fit into this established rhythm. For instance, as a parent, if a youth ministry program is changed from Wednesday night to Sunday night during the middle of a school year, that one little decision throws off our established rhythm for two nights of the week. That might not sound like a big deal, but think about it this way—you just messed with 30 percent of our evenings every week from January to May. What's worse, we already committed to the rhythm you established for youth ministry just four months earlier in September, and if you move things around in the middle of the year, you are forcing us to re-evaluate our commitment to the youth ministry (I'm using the word *forcing* intentionally). We have family night on Sunday nights, so now we have to decide whether to move that to another night of the week. The natural decision would be to switch family night to Wednesday night, but that won't work because we have a child involved in the children's program on Wednesday night. So now, if we want our teenagers to be involved in youth ministry *and* we want a weekly family night, you're actually messing with three nights of our week, or 43 percent of our evenings. And even though I'm a volunteer, I am passionate about running and do my weekly long runs late on Sunday afternoon. There is no way I can squeeze a long run in on Wednesdays, so do I stay committed to youth ministry or drop it so I can continue training for a marathon? Remember, you changed things on me midstream, so I'm not backing out of my commitment—you're backing out of your commitment to me.

Are you getting a picture of why volunteers and parents get upset when major changes are made midstream? Your one little program change might not seem like a big deal, but that little program change just messed with our entire family rhythm for the year. By the way, we get upset at any organization that makes changes like this midyear; it just so happens that youth ministries tend to do this more than any others.

6️⃣0️⃣ SLOWING DOWN TO MAKE CHANGE

The change I just described is one that I actually made, but thanks to some great volunteers who were a bit older and much wiser than me, we didn't make it during the middle of the school year. What's more, we didn't move too quickly on the front end of the process. Allow me to explain.

First off, the change was much more dramatic than what I described in Thought 59. Picture this: I led a middle school ministry at a 75-year-old church that had traditional Sunday morning and Wednesday night programming. We stopped meeting on Wednesday nights (even though the rest of the church continued with programming on Wednesday night). We replaced our Wednesday night program with a Friday night outreach program that met during the entire school year with a schedule of meeting three Friday nights in a row and then taking two Friday nights off. Additionally, we added a small group ministry on Sunday evenings.

Again, this transition was made at a 75-year-old church that had traditional church programming, and we had hardly anyone complain. In fact, our most committed families enthusiastically supported the changes, and the long-term result of these changes was tremendous growth in our middle school ministry. My volunteer team was by far my greatest asset during this change (which I'll explain in a minute), but the reason why the changes were embraced so enthusiastically is because we slowed down on the front end to make the changes. Here's what we did:

- **We aligned changes with the purposes we wanted to accomplish.** We were trying to reach out to our community on Wednesday nights, but it wasn't working because outreach-level teenagers were not consistently attending. Additionally, we also knew our Sunday morning growth-level program wasn't as strong as it could be because we could not do small groups on Sunday mornings because we simply didn't have enough room. Bottom line, we felt like we were striking out on both counts.

- **We surveyed our youth according to the purposes we wanted to accomplish.** In January, we surveyed our middle school students as to why their friends did not attend regularly on Wednesday evenings. We heard loud and clear that their friends enjoyed our ministry, but that Wednesday night was a bad night for regular attendance.

- **We allowed our volunteer team to help us determine how and when to make changes.** I gathered together my volunteer team to help determine what programming changes to make and when was the best time to launch these changes. Two quick thoughts here. First, we determined that the beginning of the school year was the best time for this change because that's when everything in the lives of teenagers and their families would relaunch for another year (remember, the start of a school year is ALWAYS the best time for major change). Second, the process of thinking through this change with my volunteers took about three months. What's more, we really came up with a solid plan together. The details of what we did are a topic for another book, but the bottom line is that their input really shaped a much stronger plan than I could have ever come up with on my own.

- **We surveyed key parents.** In April, I hosted a private, by-invitation-only gathering for parents that I knew were supportive of our ministry. A few key volunteers were with me as we presented our plans, and the purpose of the meeting was to see how the proposed changes would impact families. We received fantastic feedback, both positive and negative. Overall, the parents loved the direction we were headed, but they also helped us understand that the night we originally picked (Tuesday) was not the best night. Long story short, we figured out the Friday night schedule described a moment ago and determined that it was a much better alterative than anything we were considering. Can you say "synergy"?

- **We worked through final details with our volunteer team.** We spent another month going through revisions with our volunteer team and making sure everyone was on board.

- **We hosted a parent meeting to announce changes.** In May, we hosted a parent meeting to announce the changes we would be making in September. Overall, it was well-received primarily because (1) the plan fit the purposes the youth ministry was trying to accomplish, (2) so many people had input into shaping the details of the plan, and (3) all the volunteers and key parents were already onboard. Basically, we followed the advice John C. Maxwell so often shares—*be sure to have the meeting before having the meeting.*

- **We launched the new programs!** When September hit, we launched both new programs. There were minor issues to work out, but because we had been preparing for nine months, the programs took off! Not only did they run smoothly, we also saw significant growth immediately and for years afterward. See what I mean by "fast is slow and slow is fast"? If you want to make a fast change, slow down and do it right on the front end. And if you slow down and do it right on the front end, when the change is implemented, you'll gain traction much faster.

THINK CORRECTLY ABOUT COMMUNICATING CHANGE

Most youth leaders think through change from teenagers' perspective first, parents' perspective second, and volunteers' perspective third. WRONG!

61 THINK VOLUNTEERS FIRST

Whenever you consider changing something, think volunteers first. Will it work for them? Does it fit their schedule?

Why ask these questions first? Without volunteers, you have no ministers!

62 THINK PARENTS SECOND

Next, think parents. Will it work for them? Does it fit the typical family's schedule?

Why ask these questions second? Without the support of parents, you'll lose a lot of students!

63 THINK TEENAGERS THIRD

If you have a great team of volunteers, if you have the support of parents, and if you develop a solid ministry environment and great programs, teenagers show up!

6 ROLES VOLUNTEERS CAN PLAY DURING CHANGE

64 ROLE #1 FOR VOLUNTEERS DURING CHANGE: *INSIGHT*

I'm not sure why some youth pastors are afraid of hearing input from their volunteers when making a change; but for some reason, instead of seeing volunteers as their greatest asset during change and using them as a sounding board, they TELL their volunteers about the changes that ARE being implemented. Big mistake!

I have a key saying when it comes to leading change. If I know my volunteers support me and are onboard with the vision of our ministry, then if I want to implement a change and they are against it, one of two things is happening. Either (1) I am not articulating the idea well or (2) I am not seeing a major flaw in my thinking. In either case, my volunteers are making me a better leader.

By the way, if my volunteers do not support me or are not onboard with the vision of our ministry, it's either time to get new volunteers or time for me to leave.

65 ROLE #2 FOR VOLUNTEERS DURING CHANGE: *INPUT*

If I want the best ideas for implementing a new plan, I don't just need the insight of volunteers; I also need their input. I need them to help me shape and improve on what I am thinking. Again, can you say "synergy"?

66 ROLE #3 FOR VOLUNTEERS DURING CHANGE: *IMPLEMENTATION*

Major change always involves major implementation. Wise leaders don't try to implement the new plan by themselves; they spread opportunities for implementation around. This approach fosters stronger volunteers and encourages more ownership.

67 ROLE #4 FOR VOLUNTEERS DURING CHANGE: *IN CHARGE*

Major change usually involves major shifts in organization and structure. This creates new leadership opportunities. Again, wise leaders don't try to take on all these new leadership roles themselves; they look for opportunities to allow other leaders to step up and start overseeing more of the ministry.

68 ROLE #5 FOR VOLUNTEERS DURING CHANGE: *IMPROVEMENT*

To really know how well a new program works, it needs to run through a full-year cycle. During this time, it's unwise to do any major overhauling unless there are no other options. However, minor tweaks and improvements can be made during the initial year of implementation. Volunteers are on the front lines and know best what tweaks need to be made, so be sure you listen to what they have to say.

69 ROLE #6 FOR VOLUNTEERS DURING CHANGE: *INSIGHT*

Once the school year ends, be sure to gather more insight from your volunteer team in the form of evaluations and reviews.

Ask questions like:

- What do you think of the changes we made this year? Should we continue with them? If yes, why? If no, why not?

- What are the three best things about the changes we made this year?

- What are three things we can do next year to make the changes we made even more effective?

RELEASING

EMPOWERING & LETTING VOLUNTEERS SERVE IN YOUTH MINISTRY

Youth leaders talk a lot about empowering and releasing volunteers for ministry, but if we're honest with ourselves, we often have a hard time backing up our talk with our walk. These ideas should help you walk your talk by releasing volunteers to actually do ministry.

EMPOWER VOLUNTEERS TO LEARN WHERE TEENAGERS ARE FROM

Often, new volunteers either don't know how to talk with teenagers or are afraid to talk with them. This fear leads to that "deer in the headlights" look when we ask them to actually say something to someone. For years, I've helped new volunteers overcome this fear by having them ask teenagers where they are F.R.O.M. It's a simple little acronym I picked up from my friend Erik Lietchy that really helps volunteers get conversations flowing.

70 FRIENDS

Start by asking questions about friends. What are the names of your friends? What do you do together? What do you enjoy most about your friends? How are you similar? How are you different? Has a friend ever let you down? If so, how? What makes a friend a "best friend"?

71 RELATIVES

How many people are in your family? Does your dad work outside the home? How about your mom? What's your brother/sister like? Who do you enjoy being with most, and why? What's the best part about your family? What's something that is challenging about your family?

72 OCCUPATION

School is your major occupation right now, so what's your favorite subject, and why? What's your least favorite subject, and why? Are you involved in any extracurricular activities? What do you enjoy about them most? Are you planning to go to college? If so, what do you think you'll major in? Why? What do you want to do for a career? Why? Do you have a job right now? If so, what is it? What do you like about it? What don't you like about it?

73 MEMORIES

What was your favorite memory from this summer? Did you go on any trips? What's the funniest memory from this past school year? What's your favorite memory of all time, and why? If you could be remembered for one thing, what would you want it to be?

EMPOWER VOLUNTEERS FOR DISCIPLINE

I've led more than 100 youth trips, retreats, and conferences, and one thing a leader learns quickly when leading youth events: You must clearly communicate the rules.

Interestingly, practically every group I've led had at least one incredibly creative teenager. Why do I know this? Because if I started a trip with 10 rules, I'd come back with 15 thanks to the imaginative but warped genius (watch out if you have more than one of these whiz kids on a trip). Before long, I was reviewing a list of "101 Rules Not to Break" before every event.

All this changed once I developed the Four Fence Posts of 100 Percent Responsibility. In a nutshell, instead of focusing on rules, the volunteers and I started zeroing in on the expectations we had of students. We held everyone *100 percent responsible* in the following four areas, which we called "Fence Posts."

74 FENCE POST #1: *ATTITUDE*

I've heard it said that success starts with attitude. I agree! Why? Because, as the saying goes, attitude is everything! Here's what Chuck Swindoll says about attitude:

The longer I live, the more I realize the impact of attitude on life. Attitude, to me, is more important than facts. It is more important than the past, than education, than money, than circumstances, than failures, than successes, than what other people think or say or do. It is more important than appearance, giftedness, or skill.... The remarkable thing is that we have a choice every day regarding the attitude we will embrace for that day. We cannot change our past. Nor can we change the fact that people will act in a certain way. We also cannot change the inevitable. The only thing that we can do is play on the one string we have, and that is our attitude. I am convinced that life is 10 percent what happens to me and 90 percent how I react to it. And so it is with you—we are in charge of our attitude.

Catch the message: A teenager's attitude affects her actions, and her actions affect her life. Ergo, the more volunteers hold teenagers accountable for responding with the proper attitude in any given situation, the more hopeful life will be for those teenagers! (NOTE: I had a goal of getting the word *ergo* into a book somehow, so I can check that one off my bucket list.)

75 FENCE POST #2: *ACTIONS*

I heard Ken Davis once say, "What you believe in is evidenced by how you live, not just by what you say." Read that again S-L-O-W-L-Y and let it really sink in.

The truth is, people can yap all day long about what they believe about Jesus and the Bible, but if they don't live it, they really don't believe it.

As the saying goes, actions speak louder than words, so it's crucial that volunteers properly shepherd teenagers by holding them 100 percent responsible for their actions.

76 FENCE POST #3: *ARTICULATION*

"Sticks and stones may break my bones, but words will never hurt me."

Wrong! Soooooooooooo wrong!!

Words equal power. Power to influence others either positively or negatively. The words teenagers choose either build others up or tear them down.

If you've worked with teenagers for more than a nanosecond, you know that this Fence Post is the most challenging. Natural teen language is ridicule and sarcasm (and let's be honest, this could also be said about many youth workers). The volunteer teams I led used one statement to champion how we were going to hold everyone accountable for their articulation: *Always build up; never tear down.*

77 FENCE POST #4: *ASSOCIATIONS*

Want a snapshot of a young person's life in three to five years? Take the average of the five people that person hangs out with most and you'll have your picture. I've worked with thousands of students and one thing I know is that no one is unaffected by his or her friends. Friends are like suntan lotion—they rub *into* people.

Additionally, most teenagers who hang out with questionable friends use this excuse with me: "Kent, I'm just trying to be a good influence." When I taught lifeguard training, one of the first principles I highlighted was that it is easier for a drowning victim to pull a rescuer down under the water than it is for the rescuer to pull a drowning victim up out of the water. The same principle applies to "rescuing" your friends. For every one "rescuer" who successfully swims into a group of "victims" and saves someone, I've seen about 20 "drown" via the negative influence of their friends. A better approach is to teach teenagers to build relationships with positive friends who are authentic followers of Christ, and then help them invite their struggling friends to hang out with these friends.

78 FENCE POSTS EXPAND AND CONTRACT

The beauty of the Fence Post analogy is that it helps volunteers judge how strict or how lenient to be with teenagers in their small groups. As long as a teenager takes 100 percent responsibility in these four areas, she is totally free to do whatever she wants. In fact, the more responsibility she demonstrates, the wider the Fence Posts grow.

With that said, when she doesn't behave responsibly in one of these four areas, the Fence Posts shrink because now adult leaders are required to take responsibility for her. A common saying I used to help teenagers understand this concept is this: *Adults who are really "adults" take 100 percent responsibility in these four areas. So if you act like an adult, we will treat* you like an adult. At the same time, little kids are incapable of taking 100 percent responsibility in these four areas. So if you act like a little child, we will have to treat you like a little child.

LETTING VOLUNTEERS SERVE THROUGH BASIC SHEPHERDING STRUCTURES

In Section Two, we talked a lot about a volunteer job description and volunteer training, but that conversation is useless if we don't provide a platform that releases volunteers to shepherd teenagers. What's more, we stifle opportunity for growth—growth in the number of students we can reach and shepherd, growth in the ability of our volunteers to shepherd and minister, and growth in the potential leadership ability of our volunteers.

Therefore, let's look at important structural ideas for volunteer ministry. We'll start with some basic ideas, then move to more advanced ideas.

79 BASIC STRUCTURE IDEA #1: GET HONEST ABOUT SMALL GROUPS

Too often, small groups are nothing more than glorified discussion groups. In other words, during a typical youth group gathering, there is a "primary teacher" who shares a message, and then 15 to 20 minutes are given to discussion and prayer within a small group. If we are honest with ourselves, there is practically no community and/or shepherding taking place during these discussion times, so calling this time "small group time" is a real stretch if we truly embrace a shepherding view of small groups. Yes, groups might be small, but they are small Q&A groups or small discussion group, and that's about it. True community takes much longer than 15 to 20 minutes and requires a lot more than surface discussion around a teaching topic, even if the text of the topic comes straight out of the Bible.

Please hear what is and what is NOT being said here. This is not a slam on the "primary teacher" model or on discussion groups. Instead, it's a slam on thinking we have an authentic small group ministry that fosters true community and/or shepherding if all we are providing is 15 to 20 minutes for discussion. Additionally, it's a slam on thinking we are positioning our volunteers to truly succeed as shepherds if this is all the time we give them to shepherd. If we really want to move toward equipping and releasing volunteers to shepherd teenagers, we have to start by getting honest about our small group structure.

80 BASIC STRUCTURE IDEA #2: GET HONEST ABOUT YOUR SHEPHERDING PLATFORM

Let's go a step further. True shepherding requires authentic relationships, and authentic relationships are not developed through discussion groups. Authentic relationships are developed through hanging out A LOT, having fun together, laughing, talking about all kinds of random stuff (not just the Bible or a lesson), talking about all kinds of life stuff (again, not just the Bible or a lesson), eating together (always an added bonus), and yes, discussing biblical truths. What this means is if you truly want volunteers to shepherd students, then you need to give them the platform to shepherd, and that platform is spelled T-I-M-E and S-P-A-C-E.

Question: Are you providing your volunteers
with enough time and space to truly shepherd?

81 BASIC STRUCTURE IDEA #3: TIME

If we don't give volunteers at least 60
minutes a week of program time to shepherd
their small groups, we are not providing an
adequate platform for true shepherding (and
60 minutes is the bare minimum). Look again
at all the ingredients needed to develop
authentic relationships: hanging out A LOT,
having fun, laughing, talking about all kinds
of random stuff, talking about all kinds of life
stuff, eating together, and discussing biblical
truths. If we think all of this can happen in less
than 60 minutes, we're delusional.

82 BASIC STRUCTURE IDEA #4: SPACE

Here's something else that's delusional: thinking shepherding can take place with 50 teenagers in the same room sitting in groups of six to eight teenagers with one leader. Seriously, if simple discussion even occurs within this environment, we're fortunate. We're kidding ourselves if we think this environment actually creates space for in-depth discussion, let alone true shepherding.

83 BASIC STRUCTURE IDEA #5: COMBINING SPACE AND TIME

Combining space and time to create a platform for true shepherding is where the "rubber meets the road" as to our commitment to shepherding ministry. In other words, what are we willing to either give up or add in order to create space and time for volunteers to develop shepherding relationships with a small group of students?

In the ministries I've led, I've discovered that following the lead of what occurs structurally in many adult ministries has been a wise move. For instance, if adults attend a weekend service, they are usually involved in a music worship experience and they hear a primary teacher. If they desire deeper community, they must take the step of committing to a small group. So that's what we did, too!

We offered a primary ministry experience that we considered our "front door." This experience could include a lot of different elements such as worship experiences, games, crowdbreakers, dramas, teaching presented by a primary teacher, and even breakout discussion groups, depending on the theme of each series. However, in order for students to experience deeper community, they had to commit to our small group ministry, which was held at a different time.

The primary focus of our small groups was cultivating true shepherding environments, and we were very upfront about this with students. We said this was a step in their spiritual journey, whether they were followers of Jesus or not, that would require more commitment on their part. At the same time, we promised them that we would invest more in their lives simply because they would now have a caring adult whose primary focus was to invest in the lives of students in his or her group. Also, as I've already mentioned, small groups were the time and place that 80 percent of our volunteer effort was focused (remember the Pareto Principle from Section Two?), so this is why we were able to make this promise to teenagers who decided to commit to our small groups.

84 BASIC STRUCTURE IDEA #6: MIDDLE SCHOOL PICTURE

Grasping what a true shepherding platform looks like without pictures can be difficult, so I'll give you two. The first is what we did in middle school ministry. In order to create a true shepherding platform for our volunteer leaders, we moved small group ministry away from our primary program night. We did this for several reasons:

- When connected to our primary program night, our small groups were glorified discussion groups because leaders only had 15-20 minutes with their groups— usually after a primary teacher finished teaching.

- Additionally, the small groups were not small; most had 8-12 teenagers. This made it nearly impossible to connect with teenagers, let alone guide any kind of meaningful discussion.

- Many of the students attending our primary program were not the least bit interested in being in small groups (reasons differed for each individual), yet our structure was forcing them to participate. Sorry, but that's not good for the teenager or the volunteer!

We moved our small groups to a different time during the week and the results were amazingly positive.

Our basic two-hour schedule was:

- 15-20 minutes of food and hanging out

- 15-20 minutes of a worship experience—
  varied every week, but elements included
  singing, prayer, drama, videos, discussion,
  and so on

- 5-10 minutes of teaching—NEVER the primary
  content, but setting up the content for the
  evening

- 5 minutes transitioning to small group rooms

- 60-75 minutes for shepherding small groups

**The results of making this move were
powerful. For instance:**

- Our volunteer team grew significantly year
  after year because their role was simple,
  focused, and meaningful (see the volunteer
  job description in Section Two).

- More volunteers meant smaller groups. Our
  typical small group was one leader per four
  or five teenagers.

RELEASING

- Teenagers were positive contributors in the small group because the teenagers who committed were the ones who wanted to step into community. Again, because we promoted small groups as a "next step" in growth and shepherding, students knew what they were committing to by joining a small group. They didn't have to be a follower of Christ to commit, but they did have to commit to our small group guidelines, which I'll explain in a moment.

- We created time and space for true shepherding to occur. Obviously, 60+ minutes is much better than 15-20 minutes. What's more, we picked a time frame to meet when no other ministry in our church took place. This meant that we had more space for small groups, allowing each small group to have its own room.

85 BASIC IDEA #7: HIGH SCHOOL PICTURE

The same things took place in our high school ministry, except we actually created more time and space. We moved our high school small groups off campus and into homes, and we expanded the time to three hours!

LETTING VOLUNTEERS SERVE THROUGH ADVANCED SHEPHERDING STRUCTURES

A look at the structure we set up for high school small groups gives a more advanced picture of a shepherding environment in youth ministry.

86 ADVANCED IDEA #1: HOUSE GROUPS

The absolutely best thing we did with our high school small groups, besides moving them away from our primary program, was to move them into homes. There are a plethora of reasons this was such a good move, and all of them are listed below. But the standout point I want to make here is that meeting in homes did not necessarily mean these meetings were hosted in the homes of the volunteers leading our small groups. We found "host" homes for each house group, and more often than not, these homes were houses of church members (often parents) who were not part of our volunteer team. What's more, most hosts were blessed with the gift of hospitality, which was important in cultivating shepherding environments, as you will read below.

87 ADVANCED IDEA #2: MORE PEOPLE IS MORE BETTER!

It probably sounds like I'm contradicting what I just wrote under Thought 84, but I'm not. The great thing about house groups is we could put two to four small groups in each house. Notice what happened to our small group ministry the moment we moved them into houses and put more than one small group in each home. I won't list all the benefits, but here are some of my favorites:

- Female small groups and male small groups met in the same home, which helped us create a "midsize youth group" feel that was missing from our larger group gatherings and our former small group setting. Think of it this way: In many youth groups, a teenager has a hard time making basic social connections because the only two programming options are large group gatherings (50 or more people) or intimate small group gatherings (four or five people). Yet as many sociologists recognize, the most natural place for making social connections is in midsize gatherings (12 to 20 people). In fact, I believe this size gives more of a "community" feel than any other. So by hosting several groups in one home, we were able to add a "community" element to the "shepherding" environment we were cultivating.

- More leaders had the opportunity to speak into students' lives. Obviously, a teenager's small group shepherd was considered the primary shepherd in that setting, but in most house groups, there were also two or three other caring adults speaking into her life as well.

- Because house groups included male and female volunteers, positive male and female role models were available to each small group member.

- Tons of creativity occurred. One week, a volunteer leader could teach all small groups together, then allow the small groups to break off for in-depth discussion and prayer. The next week small groups could meet separately for teaching, and then gather together for discussion and prayer. During another week the entire time could be dedicated to small groups. The options for each night were limitless, which we found very positive because while we had a set structure, there was a lot of flexibility within that structure, which kept small groups from becoming routine and "boring" (a favorite and often legitimate complaint made by teenagers about small groups).

88 ADVANCED IDEA #3: MORE TIME IS MORE BETTER, TOO!

Once we moved to house groups, we extended the amount of time groups met. Most houses opened their doors at 5:30 p.m. and closed them around 8:30 or 9 p.m. But this is key—we did NOT necessarily add more "small group meeting time" to the evening. Instead, house groups ate together, hung out, played hoops, threw a Frisbee®, played volleyball, and did "whatever" together. And yes, over time the small group time started lasting longer and longer, but it wasn't because we were adding content; it was because the environment we cultivated was conducive to discussion, deeper sharing, and prayer.

89 ADVANCED IDEA #4: FAMILY MEALS

Allow me to share a bit more about house groups eating together. We started by encouraging hosts to provide snacks, but because most of our hosts had the gift of hospitality, they did more and more with food. Over time, most groups actually sat down around a table like a family and ate dinner together. This became one of the biggest highlights for the majority of teenagers because many of them didn't experience family meals in their own home. Additionally, these meals were the catalyst of cultivating a true "family" feel within most of our house groups and led to deeper spiritual growth in teenagers. Obviously, I can't prove that our "family meal" strategy was the catalyst of spiritual growth, but hear me—the depth of the teenagers in the house group I led went to a whole new level the more we acted like a family. And just think, this was simply an idea that evolved because we created more time and space for small groups.

90 ADVANCED IDEA #5: CONNECTION AND PRAYER JOURNALS

As I shared in Thought 51, one of the three responsibilities for shepherding volunteers that we spelled out in their job description was to pray for the teenagers in their small group. But let's be honest, knowing what to pray for is tough. Well, this idea solved that problem!

Once we moved our groups into homes and had more time, we added an element that we called "Prayer Journals." It was a simple concept:

1. We gave students 15 minutes to write in a small journal that their shepherding leader handed out.

2. Teenagers could write about anything on their minds: journal about their week, share struggles, share prayer requests—it was totally up to each individual.

3. After 15-20 minutes, these journals would be handed back to their shepherding leader.

4. The shepherding leader would read the journals during the week, prayer for the students in the small group, and even write a prayer or some advice in each journal so that the next week, the teenagers in the group could get a feel for how their shepherd was praying for them.

Again, the more we did this, the more it evolved and the more SHOCKED we became at how much students shared and how authentically they shared it. As one veteran volunteer said to me, "Within three months, I knew more about what was going on in the minds and hearts of the teenagers in my small group than I knew during the previous three years." Nothing—and I mean NOTHING—facilitated the shepherding relationship between leader and teenagers like these journals!

(By the way, these journals were NOT my idea. The idea came from one of our volunteers. Chew on that one for a minute.

The tool that facilitated shepherding better than any other tool I have ever used in ministry came from the brain of a volunteer, not from a professional youth worker. I'm just saying...)

91 ADVANCED IDEA #6: SPIRITUAL CHALLENGE EQUALS "ROADBLOCKS"

As I mentioned in Thought 57, once we transitioned to a shepherding model, we started training volunteers in how to challenge the teenagers they were shepherding. In fact, from January through May (the second half of our small group season), all of our training focused on helping volunteers individually challenge each member of their small group. One type of challenge was "spiritual roadblocks." Roadblocks are those things in teenagers' lives that hinder their walk with Christ. Biggies are things like pornography, substance abuse, or cutting. Other roadblocks are not as noticeable but are still destructive, such as gossip, deceit, and pride.

We trained shepherds how to recognize roadblocks, how to dig deep to get to the core of the problem, how and when to bring up the subject, and how to challenge individuals to break through the roadblock. I can't give handouts or outlines to this training because, as stated in Thought 57, this training was done in teams with volunteers sitting down together and talking about different teenagers in each of their groups. Veteran leaders led these conversations and also acted as "shepherds" for the volunteers in the team (if you can't tell, the shepherding model impact every aspect of our ministry—even the way we trained and cared for our volunteers).

92 ADVANCED IDEA #7: SPIRITUAL CHALLENGE EQUALS "OPPORTUNITIES"

We did not just focus on the negatives with teenagers in our small groups; we also focused on positive, spiritual opportunities in their lives!

While roadblocks were things volunteers challenged teenagers to run away from, opportunities were the positive spiritual steps that volunteers challenged teenagers to run toward.

7 RANDOM BUT IMPORTANT IDEAS FOR EMPOWERING AND RELEASING VOLUNTEERS FOR SHEPHERDING

93 VOLUNTEERS TEACHING SMALL GROUP BIBLE STUDIES

While our main youth program followed, at least to some extent, the "primary teacher" model, I would argue that our greatest teaching happened within our small groups. Training small group volunteer leaders to be good Bible study leaders and teachers is a topic for another book, but as a special bonus, you can download the basic blueprint we trained our volunteer leaders to follow. It's an excellent piece written by my good friend Chris Landford.

liveitforward.com/preparing-a-bible-study-in-two-hours-or-less

94 SECURITY

Beyond background checks, security and accountability among volunteers is HUGE if you move to a shepherding model, especially because volunteer leaders will be meeting with their small groups in different rooms by themselves. For some churches, this might mean you need two shepherding volunteers for every small group. For our ministry, we set up brother and sister groups. These groups met in rooms next to each other, and doors had to always be open so people could see into each room at all times.

95 PHYSICAL TOUCH

Physical touch between volunteers and teenagers is a sensitive subject in youth ministry today. And while this book is not the place to debate this topic, my suggestion is to clearly define what is acceptable and what is not acceptable, clearly communicate these guidelines regularly, and stay vigilant. What's more, if a problem arises, don't run away from it—RUN AT IT. Deal with it immediately!

96 EXPECTATIONS OF TEENAGERS

If a shepherding model is to work, teenagers must commit to small groups instead of seeing them as random events they can pop into whenever they like. We observed some very basic guidelines, which we called covenants. Basic concepts included attendance at 75 percent of all small group meetings and being a positive contributor to the group. Even more, when we promoted small groups, we made sure students knew this was a serious, "next level" step. This helped to guarantee that the vast majority of those who responded were highly committed to small groups and appreciated our shepherding approach.

97 OUTREACH

While this is not a book on evangelism or outreach, know that every year we devoted a season of our house group ministry to reaching out to friends. This took outreach and evangelism to a much more personal level because students in house groups strategized their own unique approach to reaching their friends. Additionally, during this season (usually the spring), instead of having one larger outreach opportunity, our youth ministry hosted more than a dozen smaller, home-based outreach series all around our community.

98 CHUCK NORRIS, TV, AND GAMING

OK, so I'm old school, but we didn't allow video games or TV during house groups. It wasn't because we thought these things were somehow evil; we just believed they didn't foster community and connection.

Teenagers grumbled and complained from time to time, but this guideline served our shepherding model well.

99 FRONT-ROW ATTENTION

The thing I like best about the shepherding model is that it provides "front-row attention" to every teenager who takes a deeper step of commitment. What I mean by "front-row attention" (a phrase I picked up from my friend and mentor Bill Clem) is that, at best, I can give seven or eight teenagers my focus and attention. Beyond that, everyone else is just getting pieces of me, or "back-row attention." But when a teenager decides to take the step of moving into a small group and if our small group ministry has truly created a shepherding environment, there is at least one caring adult providing "front-row attention" to that young person (and in the case of house groups, several caring adults). In my mind, there is no model in youth ministry that is better at giving "front-row attention" than a true shepherding environment.

THANK YOU!

In Joshua Griffin's book *99 Thoughts for Youth Workers*, he says: "Youth ministry can be a thankless job" (p. 57). He's absolutely right... **especially for volunteers!**

If you're a volunteer, let me say, "THANK YOU!" A lot of youth workers say they couldn't do ministry without you, but I want you to know that this book is about cultivating an environment in ministry in which that statement is backed up with action. If a youth ministry applies the ideas shared in this little book, youth ministry will become impossible without you!

If you're a leader of volunteers, let me encourage you to drop what you are doing right now and say "thank you" to your volunteers. Even more, let me challenge you to cultivate an environment in which ministry doesn't revolve around you doing ministry; instead, cultivate one that revolves around you "equipping, empowering, and releasing" volunteers to do the work of the ministry!

KENT JULIAN
"NORMAL IS OVERRATED"

Kent Julian is founder and president of Live It Forward LLC (liveitforward.com), a personal and executive coaching company that helps people "make the move" to the life and work they love.

Kent also speaks to thousands of educators and teenagers across America each year. When speaking at middle schools, high schools, and student conferences, he focuses on helping teenagers answer two of their biggest questions: *What should I do with my life?* and *How can I live and lead successfully?* When speaking at education conferences and in-services, his primary goal is to remind educators what makes great teachers great!

Kent calls this stuff the "blah-blah" stuff. In other words, it's the promo stuff that sort of has to be said in a bio. What he really wants you to know is that he is crazy-in-love with his wife, Kathy, and their three incredible children. One of his favorite pastimes is coaching the Stingrays, a swim team with over 160 swimmers. And just in case you want to treat him to a meal or coffee, he enjoys eating sushi and sipping dark roasted coffee.

You can track Kent down on various social networking sites such as:

Facebook — facebook.com/kentjulian
Twitter — twitter.com/KentJulian
YouTube — youtube.com/kentjulian

For more information or to schedule Kent to speak at your next event, visit **kentjulian.com** or email **booking@kentjulian.com.**